JOSH PARHAM

Stuff You Can Say Everyday

authorHOUSE®

AuthorHouse™
1663 Liberty Drive
Bloomington, IN 47403
www.authorhouse.com
Phone: 1-800-839-8640

First published by AuthorHouse 07/25/2011

ISBN: 978-1-4634-0286-0 (e)
ISBN: 978-1-4634-0287-7 (dj)
ISBN: 978-1-4634-0288-4 (sc)

Library of Congress Control Number: 2011907280

Printed in the United States of America

INTRODUCTION

Words are the paint on what we see as the canvas of human history. Because of words, wars can break out, peace can be brought, tears can be shed, frowns can be turned into smiles, minds can be challenged, lives can be changed...

The list can go on of the potential of the stuff we say everyday. If a single sentence can challenge your mind, it can change your life for the better.

We say so many words everyday, but so little of what we say has any depth or meaning.

Stuff You Can Say Everyday is a book quite like none other. No matter what page of life you're on, this book is for you.

Each page contains simple stuff you can remember to say, as well as tools to use for your life everyday.

You will find words to lift you up when you are down, words of hope when you feel helpless, strengthening statements on the weakest of your days; stimulating your mind to be challenged when you are bored, statements that will make you think or laugh-- relevant quotes about love, life and your spiritual health you can ponder and pass on to your friends, family and co-workers. .

One sentence spoken in the right season could be all you need instead of a hundred other reasons.

Make your words unregrettable and worth retelling, so someone may find them unforgettable and worth repeating.

Josh Parham

"Words that possess the power to stick in your memory possess the potential to make history!"

TABLE OF CONTENTS

"Never underestimate the power of simple statements!"

#LIFE STUFF

"If you can remember it, you can repeat it"

A person's mind can be his most
vulnerable threat or most valuable asset.

Seeds of greatness are buried
within every soul.

Never look down on anyone, because
you never know who's looking up to you!

Use the crap from your past
to fertilize your future!

If life wasn't meant to teach
us something, we would
feel tested at nothing.

Dreaming is when your heart
can fantasize what your
mind can't rationalize.

What we let life make of us
has everything to do with
what we make of it.

Your dreams don't hang on the
hinges of other people's opinions.

Your dreams are the only thing
that should suffer from insomnia;
for real dreams never sleep.

It's not about how far you've been,
it's about how far you'll go.

The hand that is dealt to you isn't
as important as how you hold it.

Your passion is your reaction to
something that brings you satisfaction.

We tend to be all about anything as long as it tends to be all about us.

You can always tell how tight of a reign a man holds over his tongue when you hear his mouth running.

Inconveniencing yourself for others with the right attitude can teach you how to be considerate.

Investing yourself into another person's life begins when you can make his interests more valuable than your own.

Some people make money; others make a living.

It's more than your income that will determine your outcome.

One good thing about burning bridges is you have places for new bridges to be built.

If you can't take criticism don't try to make a difference.

For a lot of people, criticism comes just before compromise.

Be careful who you share your
dreams with because the people you
think would be happy for you are
the ones who start hatin' on you!

You know you've met someone shady
when he always seems to leave you
in the dark about everything.

The best way to get out of the dark
is to simply reach for the light.

Blowing off steam has never
put out the first fire.

Flying off the handle will never
hit the nail on the head.

Venting is the process by which we
blow off steam in order to cool down.

People who are blind
never saw it coming!

A man who won't listen has no
advantage over a man who can't hear.

Face your oppositions and you
may see more opportunities.

Great minds aren't the only
minds that think alike.

Small minds always seem to
have the biggest heads.

Rubbing someone the wrong way may
not classify as touching that person's life.

A good memory is the mind's
present from the past that it
can give to its future.

Become the change you need to be, and
you'll see the change you want to see.

Often times change looks like
an interruption, but after a while
we learn it's an intervention.

An unlearned mind is in better shape than an unteachable one.

If the change isn't easy, it's probably essential.

Change isn't trying harder; it's trying different!

A man who won't heed his own advice is like a bee that won't eat its own honey.

Sometimes we don't realize
how much we need to change
until we have changed.

If nothing is making sense, it's probably time for something to change.

Failure is a pot hole, not a stop sign.

Your worst moment in life may be the inception of your life's greatest change.

If you don't like the way life looks, you just need a change in perspective.

What you decide in your mind will
become an inevitable act in time.

Patience is the right frame of mind
in the wrong frame of time.

Ugly words are a bad reflection
of a beautiful mind.

There are more prisoners behind the bars of their minds than there are prisoners behind the bars of time.

If you don't have a vision, now is the time to start looking for one.

Take the time to meditate…you just may think of something.

Saying nothing is much more rewarding than saying something that could be regretting.

There is nothing wrong with talking as long as you are saying something.

If what you say doesn't make someone think, then what you think may not be worth saying.

Desiring opportunities for success does not mean you dismiss opposition.

Being lazy must be the most confusing job a person can have because he never knows when he is finished.

Pride is when the devil unties your shoe so you trip over your own foot.

Grace is when the devil's
plans fall through.

The difference between being in motion
and being in action is purpose.

To lead is to learn-to live is to
love; to live as a leader, you must
learn to love one another.

A hero may take off his suit, but a real hero remembers where he left it.

If God reigns in your life, you're covered.

If your situation is getting harder, know its end is getting nearer.

The moments we are most thankful are the moments God is most pleased.

I tell God I want Him to bless my finances, then He tells me to go to work.

People who live to please everybody never really please anybody.

You can never fill an internal
void with an external thing.

Hope is never lost for those
who don't lose heart.

Hope is the scope the eye of faith
looks in to view the impossible.

Every heart that is reachable has
a mind that is teachable.

Your faith can't move miraculously until
your heart can move compassionately.

Trust is the anchor we must throw
into the Sea of Hope when the
winds of worry won't stop blowing
against the ship of our dreams.

Your darkest moments could be when
God gives you the brightest ideas.

Word of mouth is the fastest way of
spreading something that is contagious.

Running from risks may lessen
your chances to succeed in
what you're running after.

The choices we make, make
us into who we are.

Don't be who you want to be…
be who you're supposed to be.

Forgetting your past is sometimes the
best way to remember you have a future.

Swallowing your own pride will help you avoid eating your own words.

The first step toward affecting change is accepting change.

Isn't it interesting how your popularity comes to life when you die?

It's been said the eyes are the window to the soul. Then the mouth must be the door!

If you want to keep the peace, then you better learn how to hold your piece!

We must be willing to accept everyone if we want to be able to affect anyone.

It's better to have a small beginning
than no beginning at all.

When you're wondering if you're
gonna make it, don't just find
the confidence to say, "I can"…
find the courage to say, "I will".

When a test of faith has been won,
the test of your character has begun.

The down times we face are simply
reminders from God that we
are to always be looking up.

Don't try to keep your mind out
of the gutter…try to keep the
gutter out of your mind.

What you are capable to believe
in is capable to occur.

Just because a person is in control doesn't mean that he is always right, but he is always in control.

There is a big difference between caution and fear. Caution wisely stands guard of its enemy, while fear foolishly gives regard to its enemy.

A mind without repair is an unfixed life experiencing despair.

A habit you won't let go of today,
won't let go of you tomorrow.

One sure way to tell if you're
doing anything wrong is to think
you're doing everything right.

Catching a train of thought can keep
you from being stuck at Boredom.

Courage is not the lack of
knowing fear exists, but is the
lack of showing fear exists.

Imagination is like a seed that is
used to make our thoughts breed.

Wisdom is greater than any strength
ever gained by a dumbbell.

Many of us don't care to realize that
two of the world's biggest problems
are ignorance and apathy.

Recognizing an area you have
fallen short in today may help you
stand tall in that area tomorrow.

Noticing other people's weaknesses
won't make you any stronger
when ignoring your own.

Where there is no focus
your purpose perishes.

Gossip and criticism are leaders
in verbal terrorism.

Direction comes a lot faster when
you know where you are going.

Starting drama and spending money are two things humans will always do for emotional reasons and not logical reasons.

Fascination is where your mind holds its interests hostage.

Ignoring or denying truth we do not understand does not mean it is fallible truth.

Gravity will not take responsibility
for us falling in the ditch!

La unidad es cuando la division
tiene un desvio—Unity is when
division takes a diversion.

Life…it's not always what it
seems. It's so much more!

Teaching a young dog an old trick can be just as challenging as teaching an old dog a new trick.

Keeping your eyes on a goal will give you a much better shot at it.

You can find COURAGE in the middle of every disCOURAGEment.

Problems are what give
solutions purpose.

You can tell what a man thinks
he is worth by watching what
he invests himself into.

Every deed done is a seed sown.

Anger has caused a lot of problems,
but has never solved the first one.

It is easier to bow out than to
bow down. (Mom's original!)

Availability is the greatest ability
you can impress God with.

Never underestimate the power
of simple statements.

The bottom line is not
always the bottom line.

The paradox of a mystery is that
though it is unexplainable it can
be made understandable.

What's been holding you down may be the thing that is holding you up.

Being jealous of other people's accomplishments means you have paused to be zealous of your own.

Fake people are real counterfeits.

What you look at as a delaying
interruption in your life may be a
divine intervention in your life.

Just because a man is gentle and kind
doesn't mean he is weak or blind.

A problem you try to run from
may eventually run over you.

I would rather say a little bit and
it mean something, than to say
a lot and it mean nothing.

Being quick to speak does not always
qualify as being quick to think.

A bad attitude has never
been a good idea.

When you can conceive the unthinkable, you can give birth to the impossible.

Often times we are used to be someone else's miracle in the process of waiting for our own miracle.

Ironically, the people who end up being world changers start out as world strangers.

The man who had the greatest
ideas on how to live was the man
who set the greatest example.

When I have time to think about
how hard I'm working is when
I'm not working hard enough.

Your last resort may be your best resort.

You can always tell how much mercy a person has received by how much mercy he will give.

When your behavior doesn't back up your beliefs, your life lacks integrity.

A disability is sometimes God's way of camouflaging a person's distinct ability.

A man without a goal is like a
light bulb without a socket.

Mix a man with conviction,
and something called a recipe
for morality happens.

Don't expect people to understand
where you're coming from if you don't
understand where you're going.

Being derailed can make you forget you were once on track.

Rest assured the dirt you throw at people will be the same dirt you eat before or after you bite the dust.

If you like to debate over what you say is true; there may be a chance that you aren't fully convinced.

Look at your dilemmas as
detours, not roadblocks.

Common sense is a rare commodity.

Intuition is the greatest instinct
you were born with.

People who realize they don't know anything have learned a little something.

Going back to square one is better than going around in circles.

When you feel like you're in a hole, that's the perfect time to start looking up.

Jumping to conclusions can have
you landing in confusion.

Knowing you are doing the right thing
is more important than knowing
how to do everything right.

A man who stays busy wondering how
he's going to survive has a mind that's
hindered from believing he can thrive.

The difference between a reaction
and a response is how you answer.

Being still may come before being sure.

Freedom is never made without
a price being paid.

We represent our future by the
way we present our faith.

People rarely find their
purpose on purpose.

Careful thoughts prevent careless words.

It's ironic that most idle minds
don't usually have idle mouths.

To get connected with the right people
who will believe in you, you must
first get away from the people who
are draining the energy from you.

Let the time you spend on unnecessary
drama be spent on necessary dreaming.

True happiness: When no matter
what life sends our way we can smile,
be thankful and enjoy life anyway.

Relevance is more than what is
the matter at hand. It's how we
handle what matters at hand.

People don't start getting seasoned
until they become unfrozen.

Being sure of your own identity
does not give you superiority, but
it takes away your inferiority.

Whenever you become successful you
have a story full of failures to tell.

Never trust the person who is in
control of you, if his emotions are
constantly out of control with you.

The feeling of being uncomfortable about where you are in life may be just the thing that gets you moving.

Life is half spent before we realize what it's really worth.

The shoulders we choose to put our feet upon will determine whether or not we stand a little taller for the next generation.

The only people you should get
even with are the ones to whom
you owe a debt of gratitude.

Coming to grips with something comes
natural once you have a handle on it.

"Lie" is the language spoken by
those who can't interpret truth.

The questions we don't like to be
asked usually have the answers
we don't want to be told.

Learning to think innovatively
can give your problems purpose.
All it takes is a little innovation to
turn a speed bump into a ramp!

How full of yourself you are
determines how empty you feel.

Make sure whatever it is that drives you
is actually getting you somewhere.

Make your words unregrettable and
worth retelling, so someone will find
them unforgettable and worth repeating.

Honesty isn't the best policy.
It's the only policy.

The right decisions never create
the wrong emotions.

You can always see something severe
when you have to persevere.

Having joy is when happiness
becomes a habit of the heart.

Everything you do that seems insignificant is still important because no one is doing it but you.

What your frustrations resort to has everything to do with what your emotions result to.

Your biggest enemy is between your ears!

Sometimes things get put on
the back burner when we have
too many irons in the fire.

If no one is ever considerate enough
for you, maybe you haven't taken
everything into consideration.

The five senses should be enough proof
to believe a man can become successful
in multiple areas with one mind.

We have no right to criticize what
we have the power to change.

If you want to do something
outstanding, you must be
willing to stand out.

I'd rather be going through something
than going through nothing. You'll get
nowhere if you haven't been somewhere.

Difficulties don't come our way
to discourage our faith, but
to determine our faith.

If God intended for us all to
think the same way there would
be no power in agreement.

If you have to use profanity to say
it, you probably shouldn't say it.

The danger of a step in the right direction is the potential of what could happen in taking one look back.

They may not regard you when you're outspoken, but they won't remember you when you're unspoken.

The best things in life don't come easily; they come eventually.

One of our greatest weapons of self defense is to simply never take offense.

One day when I'm old, I would like to remember not all the opportunities I've been given but rather all the risks that I've taken.

Time is a lot like money; when spent it's either wasted or invested.

Don't allow a situation that doesn't
add up to keep you sidetracked
from things that really count.

Talk is cheap unless it costs you eternity.

Make sure whoever it is you look
up to believes in having a higher
standard that they live up to.

Believe God to enable you to be something more than what your past has labeled you to be!

It's not what we know that matters as much as what we do with what we know.

It may be a mark of maturity for a person to say they lack in maturity.

We make time for what
we make important.

When we are not ourselves,
everyone sees who we really are.

It's one thing to find the right way, but
it's another thing to keep to that path.

It's a lot easier to move forward
when you stop looking back.

Write a vision…it'll help you see it!

Count your blessings, not
your blisterings.

It may be a sign it's time to change
your priorities when the people
you continue to make a priority
never make you a priority.

You haven't really been given advice
unless you have taken action.

When everyone else is the one with
the problem, you've got a problem.

No man is a gentleman
until he is first gentle.

Anger is an indicator that you are
either impatient or in pain.

If it takes the approval of others to
get you out of the box, it'll only take
their criticism to get you back in it.

Time has always been more important
to the one who invented the clock than
it is to the One who invented time.

If we enjoyed every minute of life,
we would never feel rewarded.

Some people who make it to
heaven face hell here on Earth.

It's easier to show someone they
have a problem than it is to show
someone you have a solution.

Oftentimes becoming broken is the best
way to put yourself back together again.

Changing gears can help
you get out of a rut.

The career you choose to follow
will never be as important as the
cause you choose to follow.

Life is aimless to the man with no target.

Whoever you are allowing to be
a part of your daily decisions is
who has the biggest influence
over your life's direction.

It's important to know the power
you can lay hold of, if you will
just say, "My past I let go of."

One sentence spoken to you in the
right season could give your life more
meaning than a hundred other reasons.

Working is good for the body;
worship is good for the soul.

It's one thing to lead by instruction;
another to lead by example.

The process of something should never
take precedence over its purpose.

It's the one whose elevator
doesn't go to the top who has the
ability to push your buttons.

What is being heard is more important than what is being said.

Some people inspire us; others require us; and the rest just tire us.

Wisdom may not come by asking for patience, but patience will come by asking for wisdom.

It's more important to stand under
all the pressures of life than to
understand all the pressures of life.

Inspiration does not come from
information or intelligence, but
it's something like the wind that
blows suddenly into the mind.

Every time I brainstorm I'm
flooded with thoughts!

"Never underestimate the power of simple statements"

#LOVE STUFF

"If you can remember it, you can repeat it"

When you really love someone you accept them for who you know them to be, not who you want them to be.

Looks can attract anyone temporarily, but only love can connect you permanently.

If you want a relationship to have value, you can count on it costing you something.

Love is patient before it is kind.

Lust is as lasting as its process—
love is as lasting as its purpose.
Love lasts forever.

Lust can gratify you, but only
love can satisfy you.

Love that is not true is not
really love at all.

The difference between lust and
love is like the difference between a
match and a phosphorus grenade.

All some people are looking for is to
know they're really loved and cared for.

To love someone unconditionally does not look to condone or condemn, but simply accepts that person until the end!

Commitment is when a love that is found becomes a love that is bound.

Love is so hard to find these days, especially when it's sought for in all the wrong places and all the wrong ways.

I wonder how many people use the word "Love" yet say they don't believe in God, when God is "Love".

A moment given over to anger is a moment taken away from love.

No man will ever be God's gift to women, but a woman has always been God's gift to man.

The man will never receive the respect he desires until the woman receives the love she deserves.

Love is the only force that can permanently disarm pride.

Pride may bring you destruction, but love can bring you restoration.

Casual sex is how humans are lessening
their chances of finding true love.

Sex that is not making
love is breaking love.

The words of our mouths are
the echoes of our hearts.

Hope is the glue that keeps things together that will last forever.

We can't love anyone as much as we want to, until we love God as much as we're supposed to.

If love is a dare, I dare you to love!

"Never underestimate the power of simple statements!"

#SPIRITUAL STUFF

"If you can remember it, you can repeat it"

Faith is like a paddle; it rows
with the wind, against the wind
and without the wind.

Faith helps in hard times for
those who have soft hearts.

Don't let your fears take away your faith.
Let your faith take away your fears!

Your Faith in God is subject to your Hope in God, and your Hope in God is subject to your Perspective of God.

The race of faith is not won by those who start fast, but by those who finish strong.

When your life takes a turn for the worst, you know it's time your faith takes a turn for the best.

Living in the safe zone is
not the faith zone.

I'd rather be caught falling down
doing something for God than caught
standing still doing nothing.

Hope is God's medicine
for the miserable.

It's not going to change anything about God if you don't worship Him, but it will change everything about you if you do.

God has given us dominion. That is His order, not His opinion.

Just because you aren't where you think you need to be doesn't mean you aren't exactly where you are supposed to be.

The areas of your life you feel tested
in the most are the areas designed for
you to learn the greatest lessons.

Stepping out in faith means you
have stood up and believed.

Difficulties don't come our way
to discourage our faith, but
to determine our faith.

God gives more than a change in life; He gives an exchange of life.

If God only used me for my perfections, I'd have no potential. Perfection is law; potential is grace.

God wants our joy to be like the moon. Even when it's doesn't appear like it, it's always full.

God does not give His favor to those who deserve it but to those who realize they don't deserve it and dare to ask for it anyway.

Pride is the leach that sucks away the chances of the forgiven finding God's favor.

Pride is the leach that sucks away the chances of the futile finding God's forgiveness.

God's favor is not always explainable,
but it is always available.

Real significance is no more
than the application of God's
revelation clothed in humility.

Your life application should
equal your God revelation.

The best way to get out of the dark is to simply reach for the "Light". #JESUSCHRIST

The people you think are God's favorites are actually just the people who have made God their favorite!

When you allow God to expose Himself in your life, God will begin to expose your life to others.

If you can stay small in your own eyes
you can stay large in God's eyes!

To be broken before men will
keep you whole before God.

God can speak into your mind once
you let Him break into your heart.

Be on the lookout to find God in anything, and you will find Him looking out for you in everything.

I have learned that if you want to be level headed, the Bible will be the only level you will use.

The Bible is much easier to understand if you know the Author.

The moments we are most thankful are the moments God is most pleased.

The more I consider my ways, the more I consider God's ways.

If your lips can overflow with praise to God, your mind can be filled with the ways of God.

The most intimate desire of my heart
is to have intimacy with God's heart.

The world is full of people who say they
love God, but can't love their enemies.

You can only be promoted by God to the
measure you have demoted yourself.

The greatest mission you can
be on is—submission.

Miracles can appear in your life when
doubt disappears from your mind.

Fear and Doubt are the oldest
children in the Impossible Family.

Hope is never lost for those
who don't lose heart.

Broken hearts looking up to God create
open Heavens looking down with love.

God sees Himself rewarding you when
you see yourself diligently seeking Him.

Jesus cut the finish line of sin and the starting line of grace at the same time, in the same place. #THECROSS

God won't hold you accountable for a sin that you will hold yourself accountable to confess.

When you let God make a difference in your life, you can make a difference in someone else's life.

The saddest thing about narrow minds is they usually don't find the narrow path to eternal life.

You may not be able to change your past with the devil, but God can take you back to the future.

God's compassion is reserved for those whose purpose is preserved.

When you commit to God isn't when you settle down; it's when you saddle up!

Worship is not your Sunday choice. It's your daily choice.

It's sometimes the softest words that God uses to break the hardest hearts.

Worrying is the equivalent of worshipping your fears.

A relative Jesus can teach you, but a relevant Jesus can touch you!

We don't have to worry about what the future holds, if we will just worship the One who holds the future!

A heart guarded by God is
a heart guided by God.

The only way to tear down walls of
worry is to build up walls of worship.

What the world still looks at as just a
fashion statement God still looks at as
His mission statement. #THECROSS

While we think God needs to
change our circumstances that are
affecting our attitudes, God thinks
we need to change our attitudes that
are affecting our circumstances.

Sometimes we don't realize
how much we need to change
until we have changed.

The glass always looks half empty
to those who are not full of joy.

God's first and finest work was created
from nothing. That should tell us
that the finest work God can do in us
is when we are down to nothing.

Don't let the world label you
as a failure—let God enable
you to be a success!

Every time we feel torn down is when
God is trying to build up our character.

When a test of faith has been won,
the test of your character has begun.

The down times we face are simply
reminders from God that we
are to always be looking up.

When God means everything
to you, you're willing to give
up anything for Him.

If God answered all your prayers in the next month, would the whole world be affected or just your world be affected?

When we can dial up our expectancy God can dial up His efficiency.

An act that has pleased you in the past will be a temptation that seizes you in the future.

God provides escapes from all
the desires we eventually make
excuses for acting upon.

Jesus never tried to make people
feel good about themselves; but
He did try to make people feel real
and understand themselves.

No matter what your emotions tell
you, God will never fail you.

Living for the moment could cause
you to miss your "moment".

God is the love that many never
knew they were always looking for.

Jesus loved until it hurt. Then
when He couldn't hurt anymore,
He just kept loving.

If half of what we say was said to God,
the other half may not be said at all.

Where there is no focus,
your purpose perishes.

Prayer is more than a God invitation.
It's a Kingdom invasion.

To find out if prayer changes things, try doing it everyday. You will be the first thing it changes.

Of all the hearts we seek to influence, none should be sought like the heart of God.

The difference between an active Christian and a reactive Christian is opposition.

In order to receive real peace, you must first know the One who gives real peace.

Just because you retreated doesn't mean you were defeated.

The first man to ever point a finger of judgment was the first man guilty of murder.

The grace you can use to change someone's life was first the grace used to change your life.

A battle you won't give God the right to fight may be a battle that He won't give you the right to win.

Open your ears to knowledge and you will hear more than just information.

Rejection just happened to
be the key God used to open
the door to acceptance.

One of the greatest secrets is that God
does His greatest work in secret.

We can't expect God to guide
our path if we can't acknowledge
Him along the way.

When God deliberately makes you wait, will you doubt or stretch your faith?

Our answers to God are just as important as His questions to us.

A good time to tell someone that accepting God's love and grace will be the best decision they can ever make is when they tell you they have just made the worst mistake they've ever made.

When you see someone you are close to and look up to fall, believe in them enough to go help them up.

A way to tell if you're in good shape spiritually is noticing if you get bent out of shape easily.

We complain about counting the cost for something that one man paid the price for.

Be prepared to encounter small
minds that can point out your flaws
when you have devoted yourself
to living for a greater cause.

A man who likes to debate God's
existence will never win an
argument with a man who has
experienced God's presence.

Refusing to do something good for
someone can make you just as guilty of
sin as doing something bad to someone.

Windows of opportunity are
often seen when you feel trapped
at a door of opposition.

Because God was thinking vicariously,
we can now think victoriously!

Remind God of His promises
now, and He will remind you of
your promises in the future.

Trying to date God will have
you sleeping with the devil.

There have been many times my
foundation has been shaken, but because
of God and faith it will never be taken.

Take heart and know that God is
watching over you when you feel the
hurt of the world overlooking you.

Wondering what sign to follow won't
have signs and wonders following you.

Delaying to hope is to betray
your own heart.

God is busy trying to talk to us
when we are too busy to listen.

It becomes a different picture when
you put God in the picture.

We have more than God's permission
to help us keep His commandments.

Collective passion for God can cause
a Heavenly reaction for man!

Doubt is what gives God a better
excuse to make you believe.

You just never know what may grow
from one seed you dare to sow.

When it seems God is asleep during
our storms, it's because He wants us
to remember that a promise He has
given is a promise He will keep.

To be wise as a serpent does not
mean you defend yourself as one.

Fix your heart on God's promises
when your mind is faced with
all of life's problems.

I had rather be thought of as
being gullible for trusting God
to take care of me than to end up
feeling gullible that I didn't.

There's only one sword sharp enough
to both pierce your heart and
sharpen your mind. #THEBIBLE

Great minds aren't the only
minds that think alike.

Knowing what you stand on
will help you to explain to
someone where you stand.

Expect the best from yourself,
then expect the rest from God.

You just never know what's around
the bend, but first you have to bend.

Just because God is slow to anger doesn't
mean He is slow to acknowledge.

God always writes us down
before He calls us up.

Oftentimes God would rather
use a person's weakness more
than heal their weakness.

Courage is so contagious that the blood
of one man's body beaten over two
thousand years ago for the sake of love
still gives life today. #JESUSCHRIST

Anywhere you are, do anything you can for anyone you can.

Your banker could probably tell you where your heart is before a pastor could.

Feeling the conviction to do something right should be enough evidence to believe God still has something left for you to do.

Peace should be the only thing
you get anxious about.

Remember when people see you put up
a front, God sees what you can back up.

Americans would find what
they need most if they found
themselves on their knees more.

God honors the desires of those
who desire to honor Him.

God can handle anything that we
are willing to hand over to Him.

Everything may not always turn out too
good, but if you love God, everything
will always work together for good.

People who only use scripture to make a point are missing the Author's point.

There is only one thing you can find that has the value to replace anything you could ever lose. #ETERNALLIFE

Woman is the best example of God using man creatively.

Water can reflect your face's complexion, just as your face can reflect your heart's affliction.

God holds every tear you won't try to hold back.

Your flesh's willingness to submit is directly related to your spirit's willingness to surrender.

It's been said, "God helps those who help themselves," but the truth is we are able to help ourselves only because God first helps us.

The pressure of your problem determines the measure of your strength.

You are more than a piece of work— you are the work of a masterpiece.

Confessing you need God isn't nearly as powerful as confessing who is God. #JESUSISLORD

If you can be convinced you will live for eternity, be comforted you can live through the temporary.

We don't have to persuade God to keep for us what we have to be persuaded to commit to Him.

How we respond to God NOW
has everything to do with HOW
He responds to us later.

When God is no stranger to you,
Hell is no danger to you.

Setbacks are not a sign that God decided
to sit back and quit on you; setbacks
are a sign that God has set you up,
because He's not finished with you.

Guilt you won't confess will keep
your emotions in a mess.

Oftentimes God will cause a
person to be impaired in some
way, because He has plans to spare
them from something some day.

The sound of your voice is the
silhouette of your attitude.

It sometimes takes our world getting turned upside down for us to let God begin changing us from the inside out.

Life becomes a real journey when the first place we go to is the cross.

We want to be able to buy the gas, and God wants us to believe we can pay off the car.

When you feel like life is stretching you,
it may be God trying to enlarge you.

If God doesn't know you relationally,
you only know Him religiously.

While we underestimate
God's love for us, He has to
overestimate our love for Him.

What we think is the devil
putting too much weight on our
shoulders may actually be God
trying to put us on our knees.

Anger is the crown worn
by the ignorant, but a wise
man is robed in peace.

It's easier to impress than it is to
impact, because in order to impact
you must be able to impart.

The freedom of your mind is determined
by your knowledge of the truth.

What's funny is when God calls you,
He even takes your hang-ups.

The rain of fear will always evaporate in
an atmosphere filled with perfect love.

Oftentimes God is trying to relay a message to us when we think He is delaying to answer something for us.

Fear has no voice to those who
let hope be their choice!

It's improper to condemn sin if
you can't properly convey truth.

Most people buy what they
see others sold on.

A man who is only concerned
with monetary rewards will never
make any moral progress.

Taking your own life will cause you to
lose it, but giving your life to God will
cause you to find your life's purpose.

Most people never walk the line with God because they never draw the line with the world.

How full of yourself you are determines how empty you feel.

God's mercy does not give us an excuse to mess up, but it gives us an escape from ever giving up.

God is motivated by our
motives, not our motions.

Like a pencil in the hand of a man,
God's forgiveness has the power
to erase what went wrong and
start writing all over again.

It's imperative that if you want
God to move a mountain, you're
gonna have to move a muscle.

God may allow your dreams to feel endangered just so He can help you enlarge your vision.

No one can ever corrupt your character, ruin your reputation or damage your dreams, if you never compromise your convictions or give up on your God.

You can have a casual relationship with God, but it will be your greatest casualty.

Things often begin to fall into place
after we begin to fall on our face!

The reason God doesn't choose to work
out all your problems for you is because
He wants you to choose to believe
He's working them for your good.

Your biggest enemy is
between your ears!

To compromise our integrity is
to corrupt our own identity.

If your prayers don't change the
way you dream, your dreams
should change the way you pray!

Since God cannot be educated,
toleration must be His only alternative.

It will help you to know the
meaning of life if you want to
have a life with meaning.